JOHN DENVER'S *greatest hits*

VOLUMES 1-3

Management: Advent Management Corp.
Production: Daniel Rosenbaum/Rana Bernhardt
Art Direction: Rosemary Cappa-Jenkins
Director of Music: Mark Phillips

Edited by Milton Okun

VOLUME 1

PIANO/VOCAL

JOHN DENVER'S GREATEST HITS

Edited by Milton Okun

VOLUME 2

ANNIE'S SONG • WELCOME TO MY MORNING (Farewell Andromeda) • FLY AWAY • LIKE A SAD SONG

LOOKING FOR SPACE • THANK GOD I'M A COUNTRY BOY • GRANDMA'S FEATHER BED • CALYPSO

I'M SORRY • BACK HOME AGAIN • MY SWEET LADY • THIS OLD GUITAR

JOHN DENVER'S GREATEST HITS

VOLUME 3

GREATEST HITS

John Denver

Volume 3

Annie's Song Autograph Back Home Again Dancing With The Mountains Eagle And The Hawk, The For Baby (For Bobbie) Gold And Beyond, The Goodbye Again Grandma's Feather Bed H... Sorry Leavin... Space Love A... ers And Promi... High Season... ys Are Diamo... oulders Take M... ry Boy This... rewell Andro... ograph Back... le And The H... d, The Goodb... ve You Again... Like A Sad S... Lady Perha... es And Reaso... Heart Shang... ys Are Stone)... ountry Roads... Guitar Welco... Wild Monta... Again Danci... The For Baby... Again Grand... I Want To Liv... d Song Lookir... s Love Poems... Rocky Mount... s Some Days A... On My Shoul... I'm A Count... orning (Farev... s Song Autograph Back Home Again Dancing With The Mountains Eagle And The Hawk, The For Baby (For Bobbie) Gold And Beyond, The Goodbye Again Grandma's Feather Bed How Can

Take Me Home, Country Roads

Words and Music by Bill Danoff,
Taffy Nivert and John Denver

young - er than the moun - tains___ grow - in' like a breeze.___
mist - y taste of moon - shine,___ tear - drop in my eye.___

Coun - try Roads,_____ take__ me home _____ to the

place _____ I be - long: _____ West Vir - gin - ia, _____

moun - tain mom - ma, _____ Take__ me home, _____ Coun - try

Roads. _____ All my I hear her voice, in the

7

Sunshine On My Shoulders

Words by John Denver
Music by John Denver,
Mike Taylor and Dick Kniss

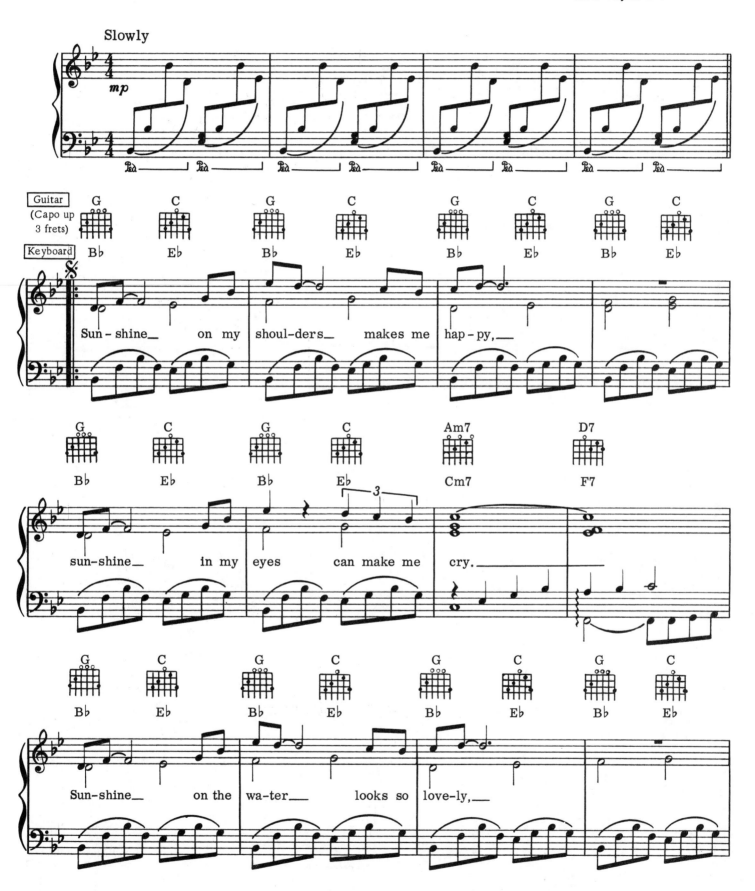

9

Leaving On A Jet Plane

Words and Music by
John Denver

Rocky Mountain High

Words by John Denver
Music by John Denver and Mike Taylor

*Guitarists: Tune low E down to D.

The Eagle And The Hawk

Words by John Denver
Music by John Denver and Mike Kniss

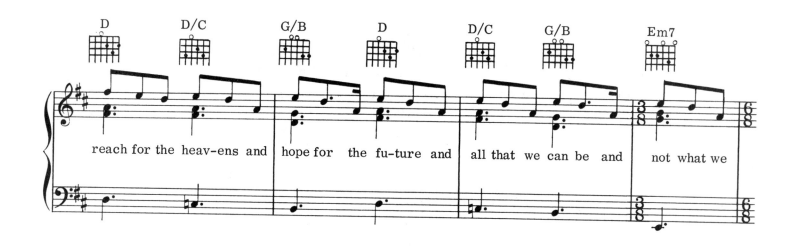

reach for the heav-ens and | hope for the fu-ture and | all that we can be and | not what we

Twice as fast

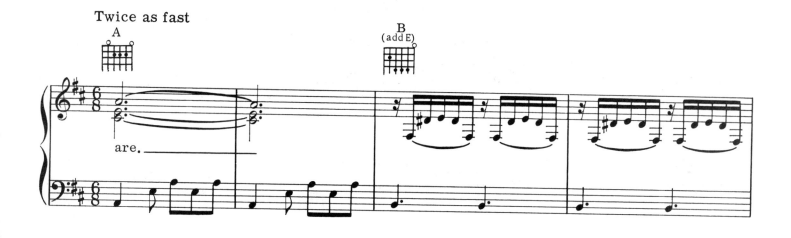

are.____

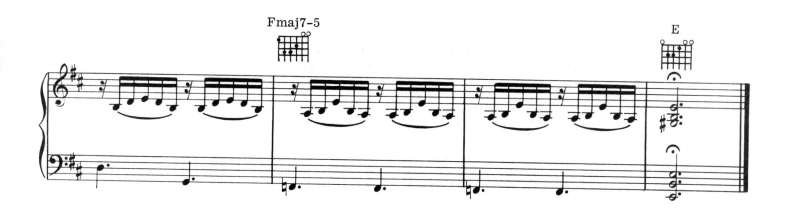

Starwood In Aspen

Words and Music by
John Denver

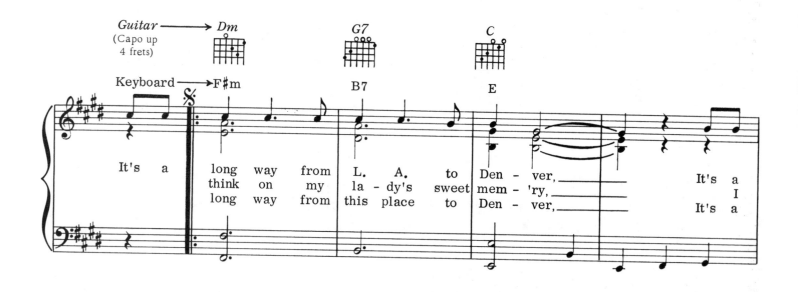

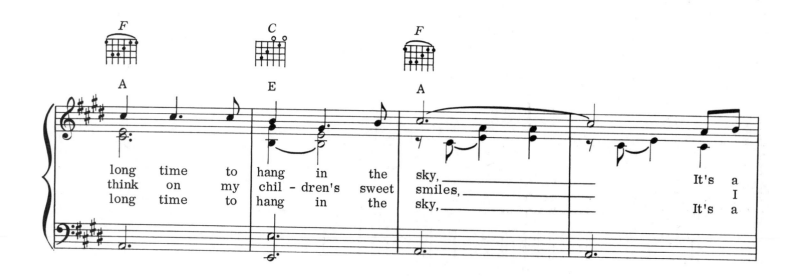

Follow Me

Words and Music by
John Denver

* Guitarists: Tune lowest string to D.

me. _____

Fol-low me ____ up and down,

all ____ the way and all a - round, ____

Take my hand ____ and say you'll fol-low me. ____

It's long been on my mind,
You see, I'd like to share my life with you ____ you know it's and

been a long, long time,
show you things ____ I've seen, I'll try to find the
places that I'm

Poems, Prayers And Promises

Words and Music by
John Denver

* Guitarists: Tune lowest string to D.

spent a time or two___ in my own home.___
dance a-cross the moun - tains on the moon.___

have to say it now___ it's been a good.___ life all___ in all, it's real-ly fine___

___ to have the chance___ to hang a - round,___ and lie there by the fire___ and

watch the eve-ning tire,___ while all___ my friends and my old la - dy sit and

Rhymes And Reasons

Words and Music by
John Denver

mountains____ and the col-ors of____ the rain-bow They're a

sing-ing____ is a prayer to non - be - liev - ers, _____

prom-ise of____ the fu-ture_____ and a bless-ing for____ to -

Come and stand____ be - side us_____ we can find a better

day.

Though the way.

For Baby (For Bobbie)

Words and Music by
John Denver

Slowly, with a double time feeling

I'll walk in the rain by your side, _____ I'll
I'll be there when you're feel-ing down _____ To

cling to the warmth of your hand, _____ I'll
kiss a-way the tears if you cry, _____ I'll

do an-y-thing to help you un-der-stand, I'll
share with you all the hap-pi-ness I've found, A re-

Goodbye Again

Words and Music by
John Denver

Annie's Song

Words and Music by
John Denver

I'm Sorry

Words and Music by
John Denver

Calypso

Words and Music by
John Denver

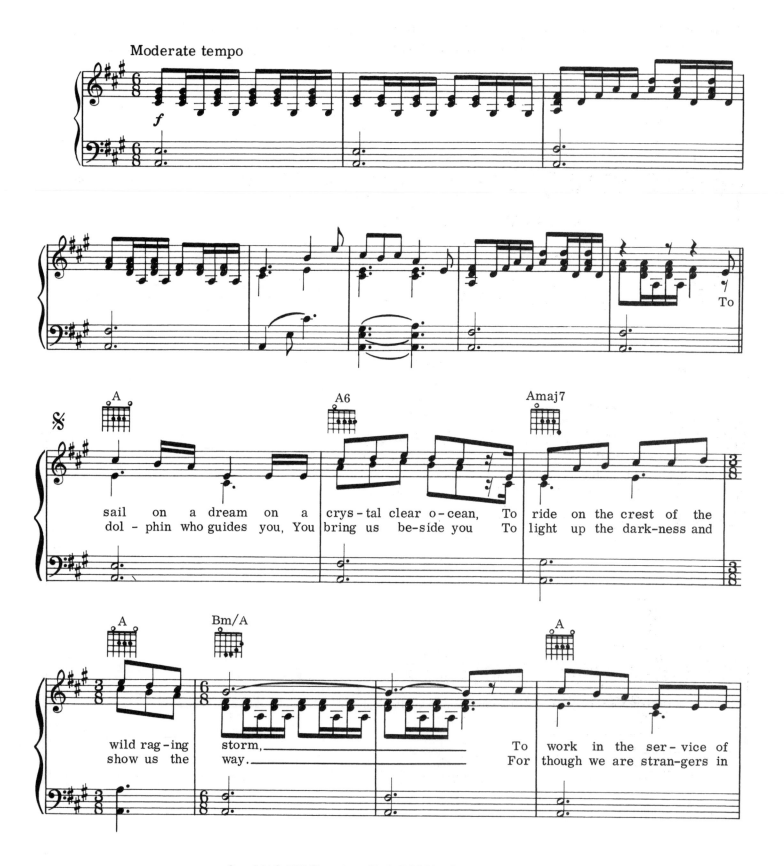

50

do-dle - ay - ee.

D.S. al Coda 𝄋

Like the

Thank God I'm A Country Boy

Words and Music by
John Martin Sommers

Moderately

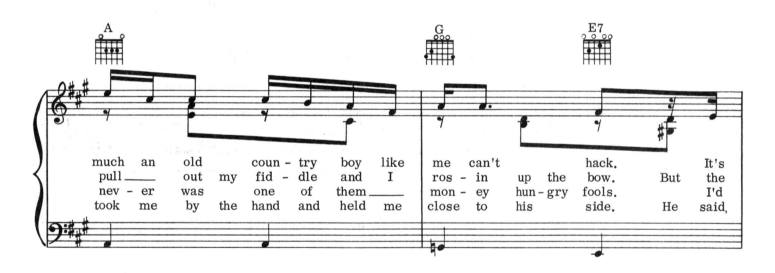

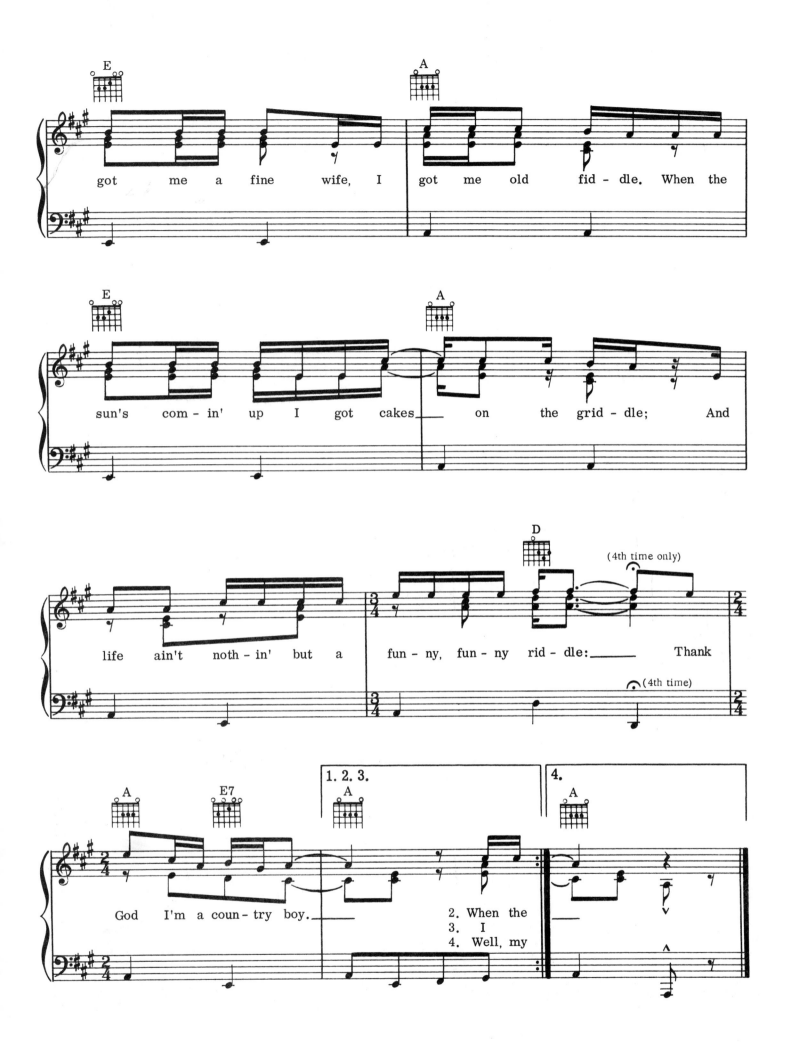

got me a fine wife, I got me old fid - dle. When the

sun's com - in' up I got cakes___ on the grid - dle; And

(4th time only)

life ain't noth - in' but a fun - ny, fun - ny rid - dle:_____ Thank

(4th time)

God I'm a coun - try boy.___

1. 2. 3.

2. When the
3. I
4. Well, my

4.

My Sweet Lady

Words and Music by
John Denver

Moderately

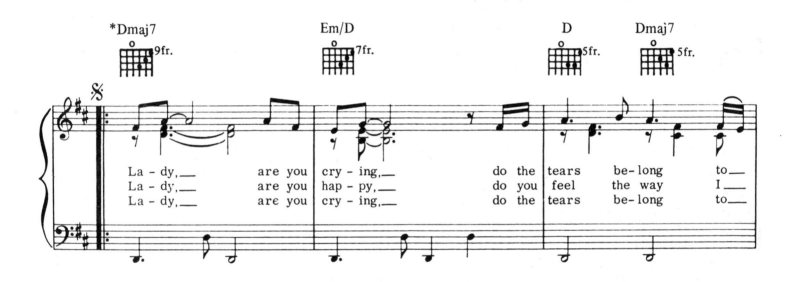

Lady,___ are you cry - ing,___ do the tears be - long to___
Lady,___ are you hap - py,___ do you feel the way I___
Lady,___ are you cry - ing,___ do the tears be - long to___

me
do
me

Did you think our time to - geth - er___ was all
are there mean - ings that you've nev - er___ seen be-
Did you think our time to - geth - er___ was all

*Guitarists: Tune lowest string to D.

prom-ise I will stay right here be-side you

day our lives were joined, be-came en-twined I

wish that you could know how much I love

you.

After Repeat,
D.S. 𝄋 al Coda

Coda

gun.

Back Home Again

Words and Music by
John Denver

61

mile or more a - way,_____ The whin-in' of _____ his wheels

just makes it cold - er. _____ He's an

hour a - way from rid - in' _____ on your prayers up in the
all the news to tell him:_____ how'd you spend your
sweet - est thing I know of,_____ just spend - in' time with

sky; And ten days on _____ the road are bare-ly
time? And what's the lat - est thing_____ the neigh-bors
you, It's the lit - tle things_ that make_____ a house a

Some-times___ this old farm___ feels___ like a long-lost friend. Yes 'n' hey, it's good___ to be back home a-gain.___

1. There's **2.** And oh, the time that I can lay___ this tired___ old bod-y down and

D.S. 𝄋
and fade
on Chorus

Fly Away

Words and Music by
John Denver

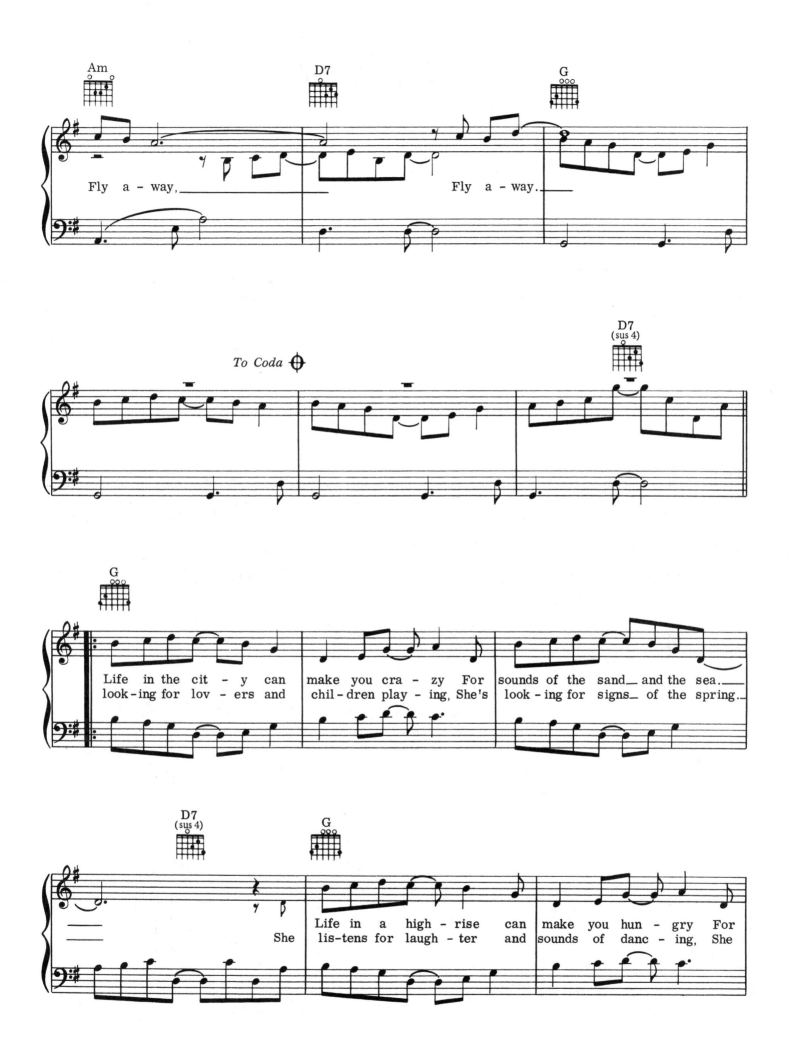

Fly a - way, _____ Fly a - way. _____

To Coda ⊕

This Old Guitar

Words and Music by
John Denver

Like A Sad Song

Words and Music by
John Denver

Still there are times when my heart feels like break-ing___ And

an-y-where___ is where___ I'd rath-er be

Oh, and in the night-time_____ I know that it's the right time___ To hold___

___ you close and say I love you so To

Grandma's Feather Bed

Words and Music by
Jim Connor

79

Chorus

Well, I

love my Ma, I love my Pa,— I love Gran-ny and Grand-pa too, I been

fish-in' with my un-cle, I ras-sled with my cou-sin, I e-ven kissed— Aunt

Lou ooo! But if I ev-er had— to make a choice, I guess it ought-a be

Looking For Space

Words and Music by
John Denver

1. On the road of ex-per-i-ence I'm try-ing to find my own way.
2. All a-lone in the u-ni-verse, Some-times that's how it seems.

Some-times I wish that I could fly a-way.
I get lost in the sad-ness and the screams.

Last time to Coda

and un - der - stand.
and reach the stars.

It's a sweet,

sweet dream.

Some-times I'm al-most there,

Some-times I fly like an ea - gle and

Some-times I'm deep in de - spair.

*After repeat
D. S. al Coda*

Welcome To My Morning
(Farewell Andromeda)

Words and Music by
John Denver

*Guitarists: Tune sixth string to low D.

Some Days Are Diamonds
(Some Days Are Stone)

Words and Music by
Dick Feller

How Can I Leave You Again

Words and Music by
John Denver

Shanghai Breezes

Words and Music by
John Denver

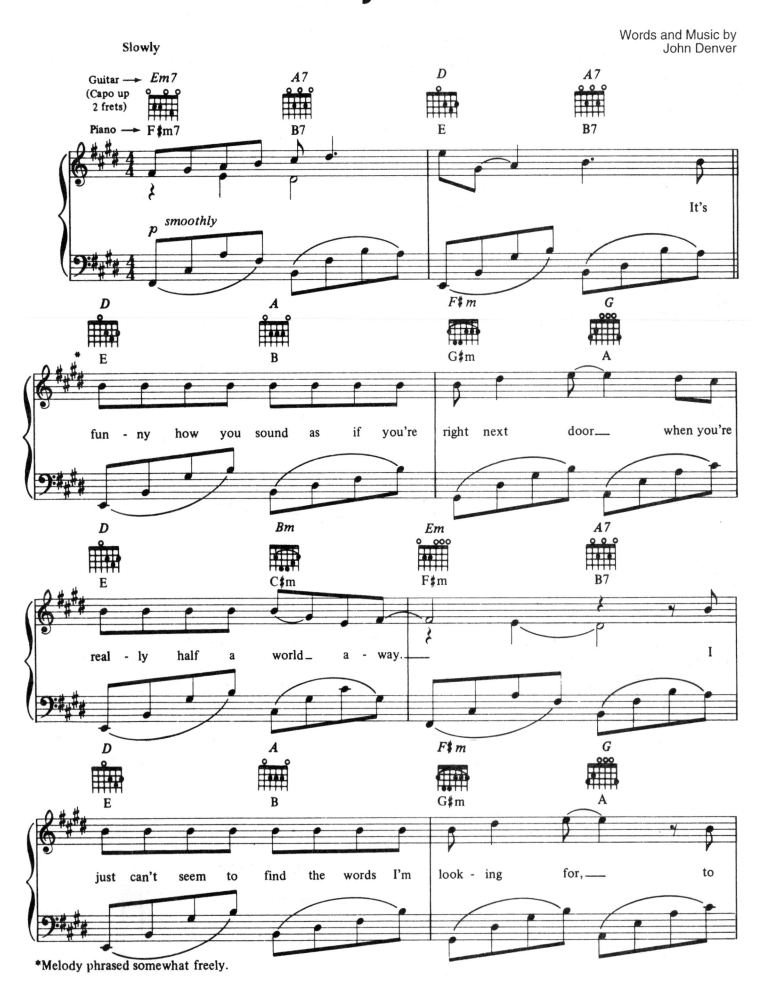

*Melody phrased somewhat freely.

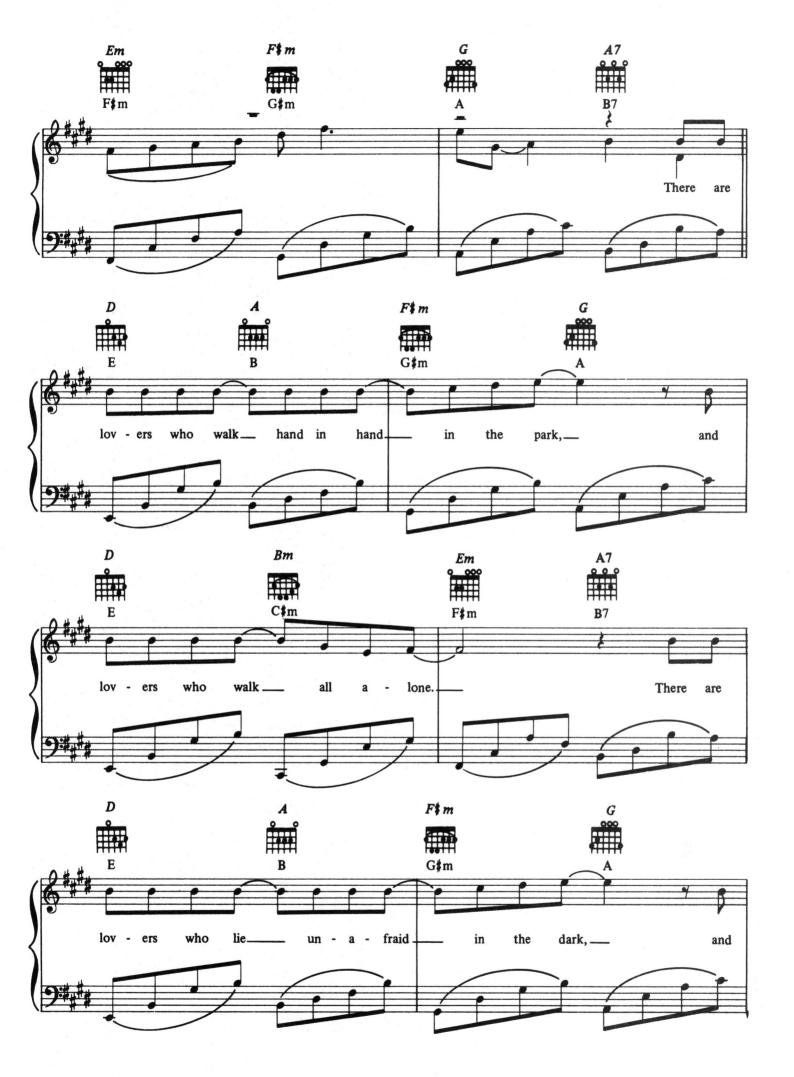

moon and the stars_ are the same_ ones you see,_ it's the same old sun up in the sky._

_ And your love in my life_ is like heav - en to me,_ like the

breez - es here in old Shang - hai._ And the _ Just like the

breez - es here in old Shang - hai.

Love Again

Words and Music by
John Denver

Seasons Of The Heart

Words and Music by
John Denver

course, we have our dif-f'renc-es, you should-n't be sur-prised; It's as
don't know how to tell you, it's dif-fi-cult to say,

nat-u-ral as chang-es in the sea-sons and the skies. Some-
nev-er in my wild-est dreams im-ag-ined it this way. Some-

times we grow to-geth-er, some-times we drift a-part; A
times I just don't know you, there's a stran-ger in our home; When I'm

(2nd time)

can't be - lieve— my heart— when it im - plies that you're not there.———
just some - things— that mean— so much, we just don't feel the same.———

cresc.

Love is why— I came here— in the first place,

f

Love is now— the rea - son I— must go,

Love is all— I ev - er hoped— to find here,———

Perhaps Love

Words and Music by
John Denver

love to some__ is like a cloud,__ to some as__ strong__ as steel,   For

some a way__ of liv - ing,   For some a way__ to feel,   And

some say love is hold - ing on,__ And some say let - ting go,__ And

some say love__ is ev - 'ry - thing, And some say__ they don't know...   Per - haps

slightly   *held back*

Dancing With The Mountains

Words and Music by
John Denver

*Guitarists: Tune 6th string to D

stretch your soul.___
Just re- lax___ and let the rhy-thm___ take___ you,
Were you___ there___ the night they lost the___ light- ning?

Don't you___ be___ a-fraid to lose con-trol.___
Were you___ there___ the day the earth stood still?___
If your___ heart___ has found some
Did you___ see___ the fa- mous

emp- ty___ spa- ces,
and the___ fight- ing,
Danc- in's just___ a thing to make you whole.___
Did you___ hear___ the pro-phet tell his tale?___

G

D

I am one, who danc- es with___ the moun- tains; ___
We are one, when danc- ing with___ the moun- tains, wo,

*Final fade omitted

Wild Montana Skies

Words and Music by
John Denver

* Guitarists: Tune 6th string to D

Chorus

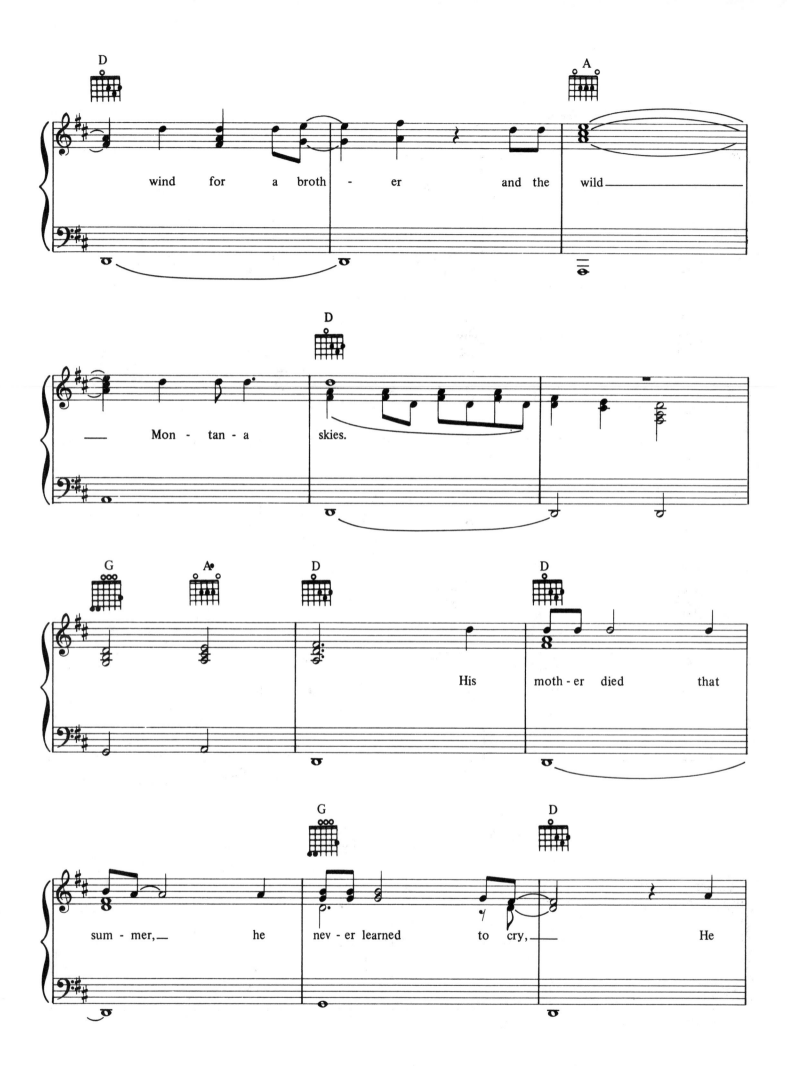

wind for a broth - er and the wild _____

_____ Mon - tan - a skies.

His moth-er died that

sum - mer,_____ he nev - er learned to cry,_____ He

never knew his fa - ther, he never did ask

why And he never knew_ the an - swers that would

make an eas - y way, But he learned to know_ the wil-

der-ness_ and to be a man that way. His

* 2nd time instrumental omitted

came to turn the pag - es and to make a brand new start. Now he
to the wil - der - ness and the land that he lived

on. Oh oh Mon - tan - a,

give this child a home, Give him the love of a good fam - 'ly and a

wom - an of his own Give him a fire in his heart, give him a light

The Gold And Beyond

Words by John Denver
Music by Lee Holdridge and John Denver

all that you can be and all that you've ev – er longed for! _____

all that you can be and all that you've ev – er longed for! _____

pianists: omit

(to Coda)

In the

dim. -

140

Coda

G

pianists: omit

We gath-er to-geth-er to face one an-oth-er,_____ We gath-er in si-lence and

C

sing for the sun,_____ We gath-er in peace to go for the gold and be-

cresc.

D   D7

G

(voice holds till end)

yond!

I Want To Live

Words and Music by
John Denver

work-er and the war-ri-or, the lov-er and the liar; For the

na-tive and the wan-der-er in kind; For the

mak-er and the us-er and the moth-er and her son I am

look-ing for my fam-i-ly and all of you are mine. We are

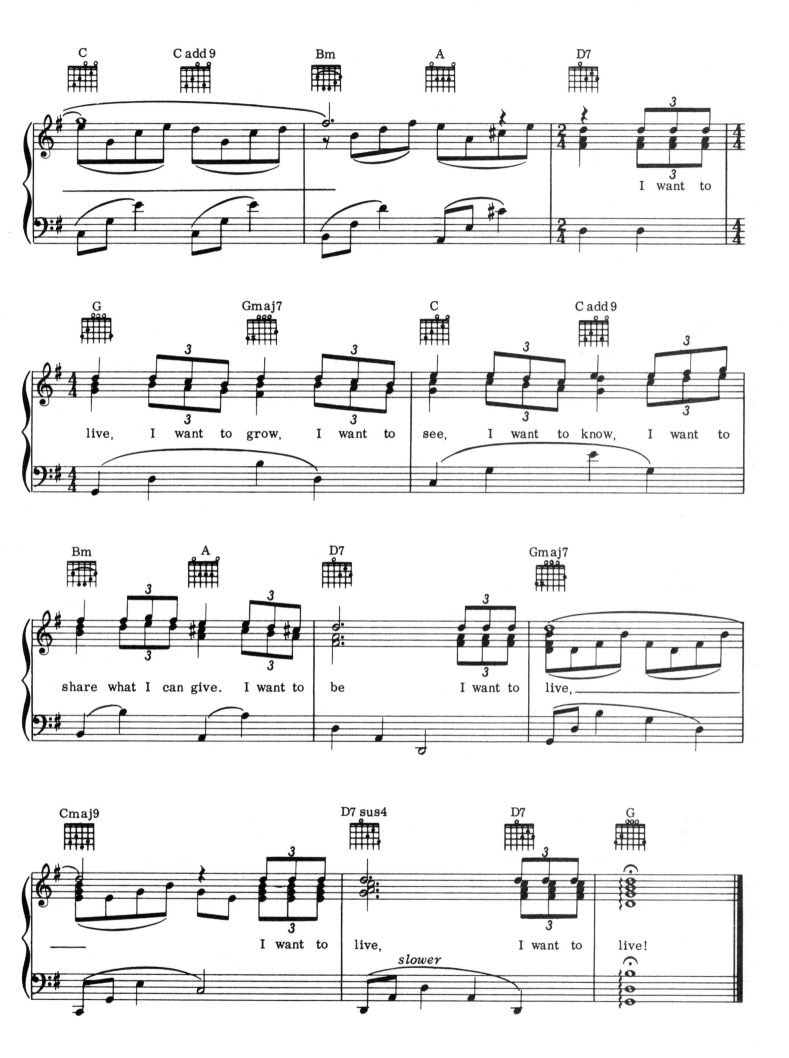

Autograph

Words and Music by
John Denver

This is my aut - o - graph,___ Here in the songs___ that I sing,___

Here in my cry___ and my laugh,___

Here in the love___ that I___ bring___ To be al - ways with you,___ and

1.
you al - ways with___ me.

2.
you al - ways with___ me.

Slower

Alphabetical Listing